TOO COOL
Fishing Fanatic

Phil Kettle
illustrated by Craig Smith

Black Hills

Distributed in
the United States of America
by Pacific Learning
P.O. Box 2723
Huntington Beach, CA
92647-0723

Website:
www.pacificlearning.com

Published by Black Hills
(an imprint of Toocool Rules
Pty Ltd)
PO Box 2073
Fitzroy MDC VIC 3065
Australia
61+3+9419-9406

First published in the United States by Black Hills in 2004.
American editorial by Pacific Learning in 2004.
Text copyright © Phillip Kettle, 2001.
Illustration copyright © Toocool Rules Pty Limited, 2001.

 a black dog and Springhill book

Printed in China through Colorcraft Ltd, Hong Kong

ISBN 1 920924 01 9
PL-6200

10 9 8 7 6 5 4 3 2 1   08 07 06 05 04

Contents

Chapter 1
Setting Sail 1

Chapter 2
Boy against Fish 5

Chapter 3
No Pain, No Gain 13

Chapter 4
The Winking Fish 20

Chapter 5
On Dry Land 23

Toocool's Fishing Glossary 29
Toocool's Backyard 30
Toocool's Quick Summary 32
The Fish 34
Q & A with Toocool 36
Fishing Quiz 40

Scott

Dog

Toocool

Chapter 1
Setting Sail

It was just after sunrise when Scott arrived. He threw his bag in the boat and we climbed aboard. We were off to catch a marlin. The marlin is one of the toughest fish in the ocean.

Scott had his video camera.
He was going to film the
big event.

Dog stood on the pointy end
of the boat. He watched as the
boat cut its way through the
water. I watched the shore
disappear from view.

We were headed for the deep sea. There would be plenty of marlin out there—just waiting for me to catch them.

Scott stood in the back of the boat. He was steering and shouting orders. Scott was the captain.

"Put on your life jackets! Scrub those decks! Smile for the camera," he yelled.

We sailed way out to sea until we finally found the perfect spot.

"Drop the anchor here!" shouted Scott. "This is the perfect spot."

Chapter 2
Boy against Fish

I moved to the back of the boat. I strapped myself into my seat so the marlin couldn't pull me overboard. I put on my gloves and turned my cap backward. Then I made sure my sunglasses were in place.

5

Scott attached the bait to the end of the line. Then I slowly fed the fishing line into the water. We both knew it wouldn't be very long before I got my first bite.

Dog put his head over the side and stared at the water. I thought he was going to be seasick, but I was wrong. Dog could hear the marlin.

Suddenly, the reel began to spin and scream. The line took off out to sea. It was a good thing I was strapped in—this fish was a giant! I'm lucky I have such strong arms.

7

I started to reel in the line, a little at a time. Just when I thought I had it, the marlin dove for the bottom of the ocean. The battle had begun—boy against fish.

The sweat ran down my face. My sunglasses began to fog up. I could feel blisters forming on my hands. Others would have given up, but I hung on. I was going to be an even bigger legend than I already was.

My arms were starting to ache, and I was thirsty. Fighting the giant marlin was hard work. "Captain, more chocolate milk, please," I called to Scott.

Dog sat beside me. He watched the water closely. Every time the marlin broke the surface, Dog jumped around and barked.

"Sit down, Dog. You'll tip the boat over!" shouted Scott.

Bit by bit, I was dragging the marlin closer to the boat. I had just started to think I'd won the battle, when the big fish broke the surface again.

It leaped right out of the water and danced on its tail! It was a beautiful sight.

Chapter 3
No Pain, No Gain

Scott stopped filming me and started filming the fish. When it finished its dance, it dived back to the bottom of the ocean.

It made a huge splash. The water sprayed all over us.

13

My arms were screaming
with pain. I remembered what
my football coach had said:
"No pain, no gain." I held on.
   Scott kept filming me.
Even though I was in pain,
I smiled. I'd probably have my
own fishing show after this.

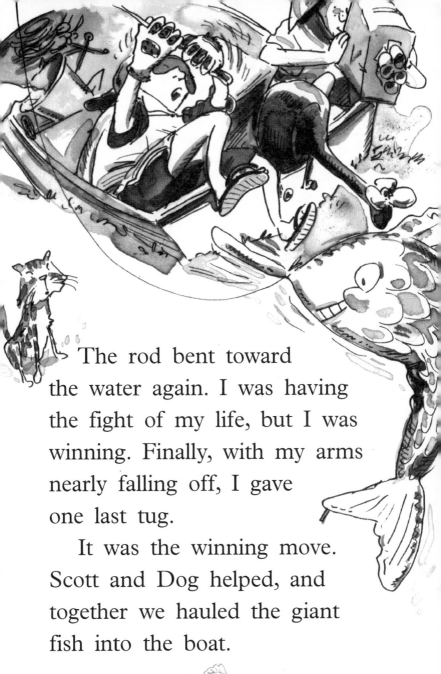

The rod bent toward
the water again. I was having
the fight of my life, but I was
winning. Finally, with my arms
nearly falling off, I gave
one last tug.

It was the winning move.
Scott and Dog helped, and
together we hauled the giant
fish into the boat.

When it hit the deck, the marlin went nuts. It started flapping and jumping all over the place! It had big spikes and vicious teeth. Someone was going to get hurt. I threw myself on the marlin and pinned it down.

We rolled around the deck. Buckets and nets and fishing rods went everywhere. The boat rocked so fast that Dog flew overboard.

Luckily, Dog had grabbed a life jacket. He dog-paddled around the boat while Scott got the net. Then Scott scooped him up and dragged him back into the boat.

Dog was all tangled up in the net. He had fishing line wrapped around his paws and water in his ears. He was all right, though.

Chapter 4
The Winking Fish

The marlin was strong, but I was stronger. I just kept wrestling. Finally, it gave up the fight. The camera kept rolling. I held the giant fish up for all my fans to see. Tonight, I would be on every TV in the world.

Scott got out the scale and we weighed the marlin. It was the biggest that had ever been caught. This was one of the proudest moments in my sports career.

Scott radioed ahead. He had to report our catch to the Fish and Wildlife Service.

After all the pictures were taken, I gave the marlin a kiss and let it go. I was sure I saw it wink at me before it disappeared out to sea, never to be caught again.

Chapter 5
On Dry Land

We pulled up the anchor and started to make our way back to shore. I knew there would be a huge crowd waiting to greet me.

When we pulled into the
dock, there were TV cameras
and people everywhere. They all
started to clap and cheer when
they saw me.

"TOOCOOL. TOOCOOL.
We want a speech!"

24

"I have caught the giant of the deep!" I yelled. "Captain Scott has it all on film!"

I started to wave to the crowd, but I was interrupted by a voice from the back.

"TOOCOOL! How many times have I told you to leave that dinghy in the shed—it doesn't belong in the middle of the backyard. What are you doing with all that fishing gear?"

Scott helped me drag
the boat back into the
shed. It was hard work.
The boat kept getting
stuck in the grass.

Dog just stayed on the
pointy end. He thought he was
a sea dog.

I wondered how many people had ever caught a giant marlin in their own backyard.

I knew I would be a fishing superstar—if I ever made it to the ocean.

Maybe I would get my chance during summer vacation...

The End!

Toocool's
Fishing Glossary

Anchor—A big heavy hook. It's tied to the boat by a rope or chain. The anchor sticks in the ground under the water and keeps the boat from floating away.

Bait—Bait is what you put on a hook to attract the fish.

Overboard—If you fall over the side of a boat and into the water, you have fallen overboard.

Reel—A special wheel on the end of a fishing rod. The fishing line is wound around the reel.

Toocool's Backyard
Secret Fishing Spot

Dangerous storms, pirates, and gusty winds live in here.

Kitchen

Toocool's Bedroom

31

Toocool's Quick Summary
Fishing

There are many different kinds of fish, but they all fit into two groups. There are saltwater fish and freshwater fish.

Saltwater fish live in the ocean. Freshwater fish live in places like lakes, rivers, and streams.

There are different ways of catching fish. Some are caught in nets. These are the fish that get sold. Some of them end up as fish sticks covered in tartar sauce.

Other fish are caught with a rod and reel. You can use a rod and reel for deep-sea fishing and for fishing off the banks of a river or lake.

There are different types of bait, too. You can use live bait, like worms or small fish. You can also use lures, which are made to look like live bait.

Some experts (like me) enjoy fly fishing. You make little flies out of things like thread, feathers, and yarn. They look like insects. Then you cast them onto the water and drag them across the surface. The fish get tricked. They think your fly is a real insect. When they bite, you reel them in!

The Fish

The Marlin

Generally blue to black on top and light on its belly.
Prefers the warm oceans of the world.

Long snout

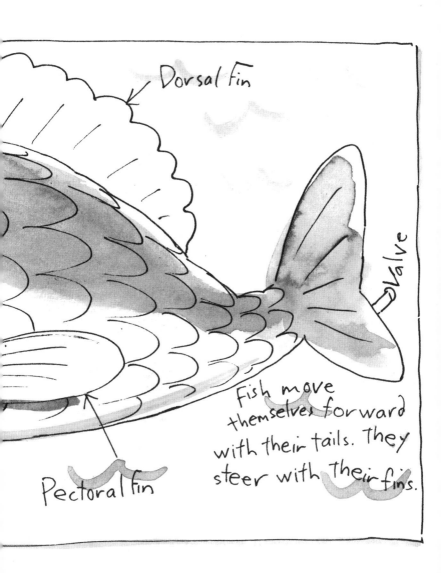

Dorsal fin

Valve

Pectoral fin

Fish move themselves forward with their tails. They steer with their fins.

Q & A with Toocool
He Answers His Own Questions

Where is the best place to go fishing?

The best place to fish is where there is water, but not at the local swimming pool. You need a river or a lake or an ocean.

What kind of fishing do you like the best?

I love deep-sea fishing. I love going out on the ocean in a boat. You need talent and strength to be good at deep-sea fishing. Luckily, I have plenty of talent and strength. I also love fishing in rivers because I'm great at casting.

What is casting?

It's when you hold on to the rod and throw the fishing line out into the water. Actually, it's more like a flick than a throw. The farther you flick it, the better. It takes a lot of skill. Sometimes even a pro like me casts a line all the way across the river to the other bank!

What kind of bait do you use?

Mostly, I use worms. I get them from the backyard. Worms like moist soil. You can usually find them in the garden. If you don't have a yard or a garden, you can also buy live worms.

What should you be careful of when you go fishing?

Make sure that you don't cast your line too close to any trees or it might get snagged. Also, keep your line away from other people. You could get your line tangled in theirs. I've also seen people get their line hooked in someone else's hat. Believe me—that's a disaster.

Do you have any tips for fishing in a boat?

Yes. Wear a life jacket even if you can swim, and don't stand up or jump around in the boat. Also, be quiet or you'll scare the fish.

Do you know where the best fishing spots are?

Yes. I know some very good spots, but I never tell anyone about them. The best fishing spots are always kept secret.

Fishing Quiz
How Much Do You Know about Fishing?

Q1 What do you do with worms?

A. Eat them. *B.* Use them as bait. *C.* Try not to look at them.

Q2 What is a snag?

A. Getting your line caught on something under the water.

B. A sensitive new age guy.

C. Catching your sweater on something, so that thread pulls out. *D.* All of the above.

Q3 What do you do with a very small fish?

A. Eat it. *B.* Take it home and hope it grows. *C.* Throw it back.

Q4 Are fish a good source of vitamins?

A. Yes. *B.* No. *C.* They're junk food.

Q5 What would you do if you caught a shark?

A. Hope it had no teeth. *B.* Cut the line and run. *C.* Yell for help.

Q6 Where can you catch freshwater fish?

A. The ocean. *B.* The river. *C.* The grocery store.

Q7 Could you catch a marlin in a local river?

A. Never. *B.* Only if you're Toocool. *C.* Only if it's a toy fish.

Q8 If you are fishing from a boat, should you wear a life jacket? **A.** Always. **B.** Only if you can't swim. **C.** Never.

Q9 If you are catching more fish than you can eat, what should you do?
A. Keep catching more.
B. Throw them back. **C.** Take them home and put them in the bathtub.

Q10 What would you do if you wanted a fishing lesson?
A. Ask Toocool. **B.** Watch the movie *Jaws*. **C.** Ask the owner of the grocery store.

ANSWERS

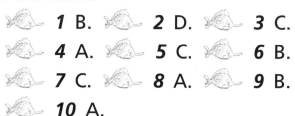

1 B. **2** D. **3** C.
4 A. **5** C. **6** B.
7 C. **8** A. **9** B.
10 A.

If you got ten questions right, pack your bags—you're going fishing! If you got more than five right, go fishing at the trout farm. If you got fewer than five right, get your fish at the grocery store.

TOOCOOL

BMX Champ

Toocool has trained hard for the BMX Championship.
The course looks dangerous.

Titles in the Toocool series

Slam Dunk Magician

Fishing Fanatic

BMX Champ

Surfing Pro

Tennis Ace

Skateboard Standout

Golfing Giant

Football Legend

Sonic Mountain Bike

Supreme Sailor

Gocart Genius

Invincible Iron Man

Soccer Superstar

Baseball's Best

Water Slide Winner

Beach Patrol

Rodeo Cowboy

Space Captain

Daredevil on Ice

Discus Dynamo